GRANDAD'S COOK BOOK

BY

SHEILA GRANTHAM

ORIGINALLY WRITTEN BY MY GRANDAD
LEWIS WILLIAM GRANTHAM IN 1915

Foreword

I have written the recipes exactly as they are written in my Grandad's training exercise book. Some of the recipes do not have cooking instructions but that is how they are written.
I do not suppose the men at the front line always got the type of food or the amount as recommended in the book but this is an exact record of the catering training for the Army Service Corps as written by my Grandad in 1915 when he did his training.
I hope you find it interesting and will maybe try out some of the recipes.
Thank you for reading our book.

Published by Grantham Publications

Printed by:
Mere Media
Studio 154, Finkle Street, Cottingham, HU16 4AZ.

ACKNOWLEDGEMENTS

I would like to thank my Auntie Ann who made it possible for me to write this book and my cousin, Angie, for finding the original in her Mum's cupboard.

Many thanks also to my friend Graham Flinton for his help and for sharing his knowledge through the publishing process.

Thanks also to Tim Walder and James Hall www.victorianschoolslondon.org.uk for their information about Napier St. School and also for the photographs.

Thank you to The London Metropolitan Archives for their research on my behalf.

My thanks also to Trevor Poole and the re-enactors of the Great War Society for allowing me use their photographs portraying the equipment and uniforms as used by my Grandfather.

Thank you also to Charles Dinsdale and Frank Rutland, two very kind and helpful gentlemen of The Hull Peoples Memorial in Whitefriargate, Hull.

My main thanks are respectfully given to Lewis William for his part in the Great War, to his brother Harry Robinson and to all members of the forces and the civilians who fought so bravely and to the many who gave their health, their sanity and in so many cases their lives.

They will never be forgotten.

The Grantham Family Timeline

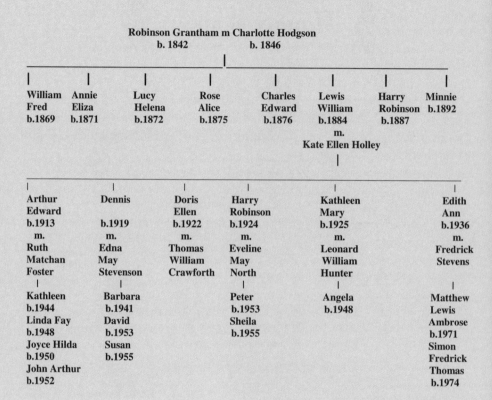

Robinson Grantham m Charlotte Hodgson
b. 1842   b. 1846

| William Fred b.1869 | Annie Eliza b.1871 | Lucy Helena b.1872 | Rose Alice b.1875 | Charles Edward b.1876 | Lewis William b.1884 m. Kate Ellen Holley | Harry Robinson b.1887 | Minnie b.1892 |

| Arthur Edward b.1913 m. Ruth Matchan Foster | Dennis b.1919 m. Edna May Stevenson | Doris Ellen b.1922 m. Thomas William Crawforth | Harry Robinson b.1924 m. Eveline May North | Kathleen Mary b.1925 m. Leonard William Hunter | Edith Ann b.1936 m. Fredrick Stevens |
| Kathleen b.1944 Linda Fay b.1948 Joyce Hilda b.1950 John Arthur b.1952 | Barbara b.1941 David b.1953 Susan b.1955 | | Peter b.1953 Sheila b.1955 | Angela b.1948 | Matthew Lewis Ambrose b.1971 Simon Fredrick Thomas b.1974 |

4

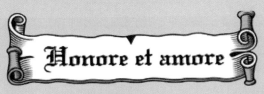

Honore et amore

Grantham

The Early Days Together.

Lewis and Kate possibly on their wedding day.
1st March 1913

Lewis William Grantham

Lewis William was born on the 1st of July 1884. He was one of 8 children to Robinson and Charlotte. He was born in the village of Aldbrough, East Riding of Yorkshire.

Lewis went to the local school, although probably not as often as he should. On March 31st 1898 Lewis and his brother Harry had been absent from school for the greater part of the week and were reminded that according to the bye laws of the School Attendance Committee of the Skirlaugh Union they must make at least 25 appearances a month. I think by this time Lewis was of school leaving age. His brother Harry was 11. Much of the time taken off school was probably to enable them to work on the land.

Robinson was a farm labourer for most of his life but in 1882 at the time of Minnie's birth he was a "Beer Keeper" at The Elm Tree Inn in Aldbrough. He was still doing this in 1897. Robinson died in 1913 aged 72. Charlotte died in 1923 aged 76.

At the age of 28 on the 1st of March 1913 Lewis married Kate Ellen Holley at St. Peters church in Bilton, East Yorkshire. Lewis and Kate remained in Bilton for the rest of Lewis's life.

He worked on the land and with horses, his favourite of all animals. Lewis was a quiet, private man who enjoyed his woodbines and a pint of Guinness. He was a hard worker and kept an allotment for many years. He was strict with his children and expected his rules to be followed. I think Lewis was a typical man of his generation. He always wore his soft flannelette shirts with removable collars, his braces and a waistcoat (usually having a packet of mints in his pocket).

Although he was quite a serious, strict man he did however possess a wicked sense of humour. One day he had been working on his allotment when he came rushing into the house, taking Ann, his youngest daughter outside to the village hall. He was rolling with laughter as they listened to the ladies of the local W.I choir singing "Jack and Jill".

They were obviously practising something or other but Lewis found it highly amusing that "grown women were singing little kids nursery rhymes".

He didn't find it quite so funny when my dad (Harry) put price tickets on the neighbours washing and made a sign for a Jumble Sale with an arrow pointing down to the back yards where the washing was blowing in the breeze. I don't know if any of the washing was sold or if my dad made any money but I do think he would have suffered his dad's wrath and probably couldn't sit down for a week.

Lewis was very particular about his boots and shoes, even polishing the soles to preserve the leather. He continued to wear his hob nail boots until the time he was bedbound.

He also took on the role of polishing all the family's boots and shoes. Lewis became a gardener/handyman for a local business man with Kate working as their cleaner.

The children of the family couldn't pronounce the name Grantham so Lewis and Kate became known as Mr and Mrs Bambin. The family presented them with a goose every Christmas.

Lewis and Kate also cleaned the old village hall in Bilton for many years.

Lewis remained a keen gardener and a lover of horses all his life. He also continued to do much of the cooking at home using some of the recipes in his ASC training book.

The family favourites being liver and onions with onion gravy and marrowbone broth with lots of his home grown veg and suet dumplings. Mince was another of his culinary masterpieces.

I do not know much about my Grandad's military service, only what I can make out from his records. It is a shame that when older relatives are still with us we are too young to be interested in their experiences. When we are it is usually too late. My Grandad died in 1963 when I was 8 years old so questions about what he did in the 1st world war were the last thing on my mind. I do remember however that he was an excellent gardener and he made the best pickled onions I have ever tasted. I also remember he had a glass eye (lost to glaucoma) which he kept in a glass of water by his bedside.

He had a bed in the living room in his latter years after having a stroke. He also suffered with pneumonia on more than one occasion. His recipe book is one of the few remaining items from his war time experience as sometime after the war he burnt everything else including photographs and the many silk postcards which he sent to Kate from France. I think the reason he kept the book is that it was of use to him in civilian life.

On the 28th December 1914 Lewis went for his medical prior to his enlistment.
He passed and on the 4th of January 1915 he applied to join the army at the West Hull Recruitment Office which was based in the City Hall. His application was approved on the 6th of January.
His first inoculation was on the 12th of March and the second on the 25th, with a vaccination on the 12th of April. Lewis joined the A.S.C 23rd Divisional Train, 193 Company.
He was now Private Lewis William Grantham, Reg. no. 036977. He was assigned to No.4 HT depot which was a horse transport depot based at Bradford.
During the months between April and August he was doing his training.
Lewis was a driver in the horse transport. He would have been happy to be back working with his favourite animals. He was also given the job of "cook".
I believe that Lewis's catering training was done at The London Napier Street School. The only reason I have for thinking this is that the name "Napier Street School" is hand written by Lewis on the front cover. I have made enquiries but can find nothing saying the school was used by the army during WW1. The school's log books and registers are not available to the public until 2017.
I am not a military historian but have tried to make sure that any information in the book is true and exact.
During Lewis's time overseas his company were involved in much of the fighting. I do not know every battle in which he was involved so I have tried to ensure the following information is as correct as possible.

Photographs of Napier Street School.

The School was built in 1885 and since 1951 has been called The Thomas Fairchild Community School. The old school was burnt down in 2009 and a new one was built in its place.

Photos taken by James Hall. www.victorianschoolslondon.org.uk

Lewis embarked aboard the Queen Alexandra in Southampton on the 25th August 1915 headed for France. He disembarked in Havre on the 28th.

In September 1915 the 23rd Division were moved to the Merris-Vieux Berqiun area for trench familiarization.

Just nine days later the Division were responsible for a section of the front line between Ferme Grande Flamengrie to the Armentieries-Wez Maquart road. At the time of the battle of Loos the 23rd Division were holding the front line at Bois Grenier. They remained in this area for quite a while. They were relieved of this position in late January to early February 1916 after five long months. In early March they were ordered to move to the Carency Sector. They held the front between Boyau de l'Ersatz and the Souchez River. The area suffered extreme shelling. In April the Division were relieved and moved back to the Bruay area.

Lewis was admitted to hospital on the 3rd April 1916 and discharged on the 6th, he was also admitted on a few other occasions for various ailments.

In May they moved again back to the Souchez-Angres front.

Then on 21st May came the German attack on Vimy Ridge, which was to the right of the Division's position. The area suffered severe shelling. On 31st May Lewis was granted leave until 7th June. The Division were relieved on 11th June, moving on to Bomy, where they took part in extensive training ready for what was still to come.

The 23rd Division took part in the following battles but as I said I do not know for sure if Grandad was involved in them all.

On the 1st July 1916, Lewis's 32nd birthday he was involved in the battle of Albert, the first day of fighting on the Somme.

The Battle of Vimy Ridge
The Battle of Albert (Contalmaison was captured by the 23rd division).
Bazantin
Pozieres
Flers-Courcelette
Morval

Le Transloy (Le Sars was captured by the 23rd division).
Messines
Mennin Road (Ypres)
Polygon Wood   ``
Passchendaele (1st and 2nd Battles)

Lewis was granted leave from 6th August 1917 until 16th.
In October 1917 the Division were moved to Italy and were involved
in the battles of Asiago and Vittorio Veneto. Also the battle for the
Pass of Piave and of Monticano.
The 23rd Division remained in Italy for the remainder of the war.
In Italy the armistice took place on 4th November 1918 at 3pm. At
that time the Division were halfway between the rivers Livenza and
Meduna.
Late November 1918 he was transferred to the 2nd Company, 48th
Division (a motorized transport division). On 12th December he was
transferred to the 3rd Company and then on 29th December he was
back with his 4th Company.
In March 1919 Lewis was back in Britain at an army camp in Ripon.
He was demobbed to Class Z Army Reserve on 29th June 1919.

During the war The 23rd Division suffered over 23,000 casualties,
killed, wounded or missing.

On the 26th of January 1917 Lewis was awarded the Good Conduct Badge (an inverted stripe on the left cuff, given after 2 years service).

At the end of the war Lewis was awarded The 1914/15 Star, The British War Medal and The Victory Medal. This trio of commemorative medals were issued to members of the forces who had served in the Great War. The medals became known as Pip, Squeak and Wilfred. They were given these names after characters in a comic strip in the Daily Mail. The strip first appeared in May 1919 and became extremely popular around the time that the medals were being issued.

The character Pip was a dog, Squeak a penguin and Wilfred a rabbit. The 1914/15 Star was Pip, Squeak was The British War Medal and The 1914 to 1919 Victory Medal was Wilfred.

According to my father, when Lewis was on his deathbed he claimed that he could see his old Commanding Officer waiting and calling out for him. Such was the impact the Great War must have had on my granddad, Lewis William Grantham.

In July 1916 all soldiers were issued with two identification tags, one red and one green. The tags were made of compressed fibre and were worn round the neck on a length of butchers twine. In case of a fatality one tag stayed with the body and the other one went to the person in charge of burials for record keeping purposes.
In 1918 a serial number system was used instead.

Here are Lewis's I.D tags and also his original ASC cap badge. Here also is Lewis's one remaining Medal. It is the Victory Medal although it is on the wrong ribbon.

The brass tin known as the Queen Mary Christmas Tin was sent to anyone serving overseas in the armed forces at Christmas 1914. The idea for the tins came from 17 year old Princess Mary, daughter of George V and Queen Mary, as a gift from the nation. She had earlier set up The Soldier and Sailors Fund. The tins contained a pipe, 1 oz tobacco, twenty cigarettes and a lighter for the smokers. Non smokers and boys received a bullet pencil and some sweets in their tins.

I believe this tin would have belonged to Lewis's brother, Harry serving in the Royal Navy as Lewis was not overseas until 1915.

Army Form B. 2505

SHORT SERVICE.

(For the Duration of the War.)

ATTESTATION OF

No. ___ Name ___ Corps ___

Questions to be put to the Recruit before enlistment.

1.	What is your Name?	Lewis William Grantham
2.	What is your full Address?	Carlton Lane Aldbrough near Hull
3.	Are you a British Subject?	Yes
4.	What is your Age?	30 Years 5 Months
5.	What is your Trade or Calling?	Farm Servant
6.	Are you Married?	Yes
7.	Have you ever served in any branch of His Majesty's Forces, naval or military; if so, which?	No
8.	Are you willing to be vaccinated or re-vaccinated?	Yes
9.	Are you willing to be enlisted for General Service?	Yes
10.	Did you receive a Notice, and do you understand its meaning, and who gave it to you?	Yes, Sgt Taylor Corps 2 Northn R.F.A.
11.	Are you willing to serve upon the following conditions...	Yes

I, Lewis William Grantham, do solemnly declare that the above answers made by me to the above questions are true...

Lewis William Grantham

SIGNATURE OF RECRUIT

Sgt Taylor Sgt — Signature of Witness

OATH TO BE TAKEN BY RECRUIT ON ATTESTATION

I, Lewis William Grantham, swear by Almighty God, that I will be faithful and bear true Allegiance to His Majesty King George the Fifth...

CERTIFICATE OF MAGISTRATE OR ATTESTING OFFICER

WEST HULL R.O.

Signature of Justice

Certificate of Approving Officer

Date 6.1.15
Place Bradford

Appearing Officer

16

Army Form B. 178.

To be used for recruits enlisting direct into the Regular Army only.
Army Form B. 178ᵃ to be used for Special Reserve recruits and
Special Reservists enlisting into the Regular Army.

MEDICAL HISTORY of

03/977

Surname **Grantham**   Christian Name **Lewis William**

TABLE I.—GENERAL TABLE

Birthplace ... Parish	Aldbrough	County Yorks

on 2? day of December 1914

Examined ...   West Hull R.O.

Declared Age ... 30   days.

Trade or Occupation ...

Height ... feet inches.

Weight ... 139 lbs.

Chest Measurement {Girth when fully Expanded / Range of Expansion} ... 2 inches.

Physical Development ... Good

Vaccination Marks {Arm / Number}

When Vaccinated ... Infancy

Vision ... R.E.—V normal L.E.—V normal

(a) Marks indicating congenital peculiarities or previous disease ... (a)

(b) Slight defects but not sufficient to cause rejection ... (b)

Approved by ... (Signature)   Wm. A. Thompson

(Rank)   Major   Medical Officer.

Enlisted ...   WEST HULL R.O.
on fourth day of 1915

Joined on Enlistment

	Corps.	Regtl. No.
Transferred to	A S C	M/036407

Became non-effective by ...

on day of 19

(Signature)

Table III.—Boards; Courts of Inquiry, Vaccination, Inoculations, &c.; Examinations for Field or Foreign Service; Extension, Re-engagement, or Prolongation of Service; Issue of Surgical Appliances; Particulars of Dental Treatment, &c.

Date.	Brief details, and signature.

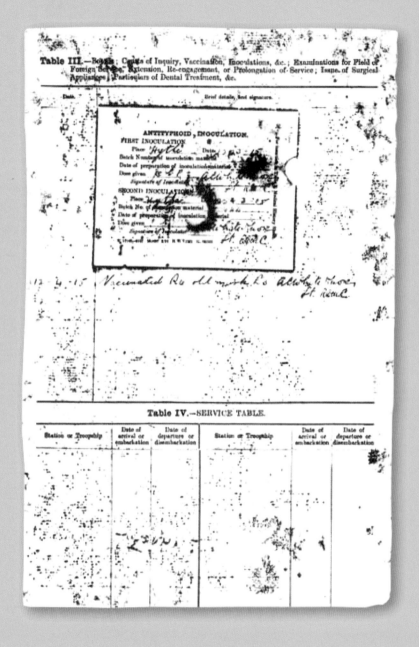

ANTITYPHOID INOCULATION.

FIRST INOCULATION.
Place _Hythe_   Date
Batch Number of inoculation material
Date of preparation of inoculation material
Dose given
Signature of Inoculator

SECOND INOCULATION.
Place
Batch No. of inoculation material
Date of preparation of inoculation material
Dose given
Signature of Inoculator

12-4-15   Vaccinated Re all marks Rs allthytic Twores
H. CoatC

Table IV.—SERVICE TABLE.

Station or Troopship	Date of arrival or embarkation	Date of departure or disembarkation	Station or Troopship	Date of arrival or embarkation	Date of departure or disembarkation

Army Form B. 103.

Casualty Form—Active Service.

Regiment or Corps _____

Regimental No.	Rank	Name
216927	Pte	Bradshaw, R...

Enlisted (a) _____ Terms of Service (a) _____ Date of appointment _____ Service reckons from (a) _____

Date of promotion to present rank _____ to lance rank _____ Numerical position on roll of N.C.Os. _____

Date	Report		Place	Date	Remarks	
	From whom received				taken from Army Form B. 213, Army Form A. 36, or other official documents	

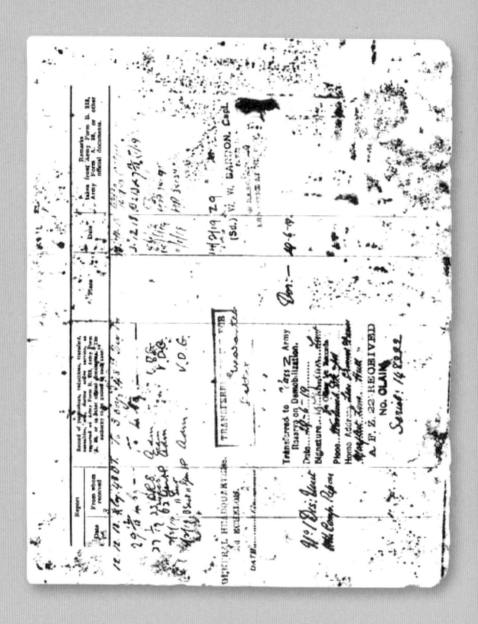

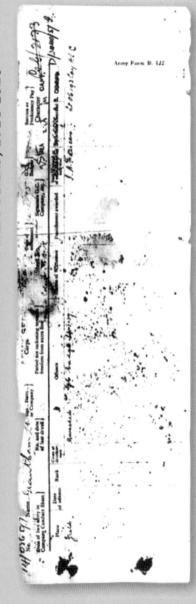

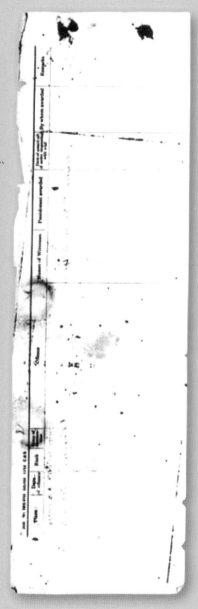

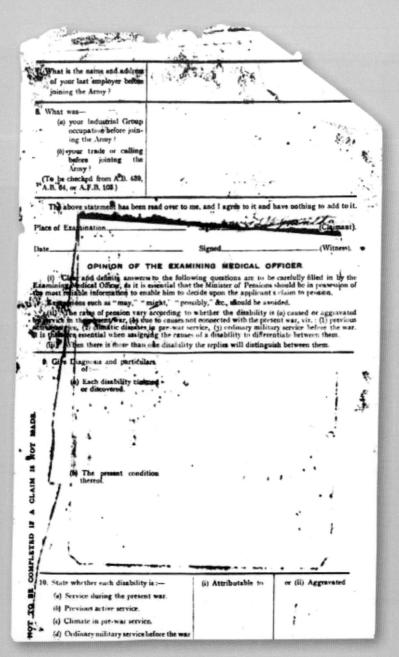

| 7. What is the name and address of your last employer before joining the Army? | |
| 8. What was— (a) your Industrial Group occupation before joining the Army? (b) your trade or calling before joining the Army? (To be checked from A.B. 439, A.B. 64, or A.F.B. 103) | |

The above statement has been read over to me, and I agree to it and have nothing to add to it.

Place of Examination _____ _____ (Claimant).

Date _____ Signed _____ (Witness).

OPINION OF THE EXAMINING MEDICAL OFFICER.

(i) Clear and definite answers to the following questions are to be carefully filled in by the Examining Medical Officer, as it is essential that the Minister of Pensions should be in possession of the most reliable information to enable him to decide upon the applicant's claim to pension. Expressions such as "may," "might," "possibly," &c., should be avoided.

(ii) The rates of pension vary according to whether the disability is (a) caused or aggravated by service in the present war, (b) due to causes not connected with the present war, viz. : (1) previous active service, (2) climatic diseases in pre-war service, (3) ordinary military service before the war. It is therefore essential when assigning the causes of a disability to differentiate between them.

(iii) When there is more than one disability the replies will distinguish between them.

9. Give Diagnosis and particulars of :—

(a) Each disability claimed or discovered.

(b) The present condition thereof.

10. State whether each disability is :—	(i) Attributable to	or (ii) Aggravated
(a) Service during the present war.		
(b) Previous active service.		
(c) Climate in pre-war service.		
(d) Ordinary military service before the war		

NOT TO BE COMPLETED IF A CLAIM IS NOT MADE.

23

☞ IF FOUND, please drop this Certificate in a Post Office letter box.　Army Form Z. 11.

NOTICE.—"This document is Government property. It is no security whatever for debt, and any Person being in possession of it, either as a pledge or security for debt, or without lawful authority or excuse, is liable under Section 156 (9) of the Army Act to a fine of twenty pounds (£20) or imprisonment for six months, or to both fine and imprisonment."

PROTECTION CERTIFICATE AND CERTIFICATE OF IDENTITY

SOLDIER NOT REMAINING WITH THE COLOURS

Dispersal Unit Stamp and date of dispersal

L45.

Surname _GRANTHAM_
(Block letters)

Christian Names _LEWIS WILLIAM_

Regtl. No. _036771_　Rank _Pt_　Record Office _Woolwich_

Unit _2 Batt Depot R.F.A._　Regt. or Corps _R. F. A._　Pay Office _____

I have received an advance of £2.　† Address for Pay _Four Grounds Farm_

(Signature of Soldier) _____　_____ Hill

The above-named soldier is granted 28 days' furlough from the date stamped hereon pending (or so far as can be ascertained) which will date from the last day of furlough after which date uniform will not be worn except upon occasions authorized by Army Orders.

*If for Final Demobilisation insert 1.
If embodiment insert 2.
Transfer to Reserve insert 3.

Theatre of War or Command _Italy_

Born in the Year _1883_

Medical Category _____

Place of rejoining in case of emergency _____

Specialist Military Qualification _____

'25
456

† As this is the address to which pay and discharge documents will be sent unless further notification is received, any change of address must be reported at once to the Record Office and the Pay Office as noted above, otherwise delay in settlement will occur.

This Certificate must be produced when applying for an Unemployed Sailor's and Soldier's Donation Policy or, if demanded, whenever applying for Unemployment benefit.

Date _11/6/19_　Office of Issue _Ripon_　Policy issued No. _____

Dis: Branch　Transferred to Z
Entered on alt:　on 29-6-19　(3)

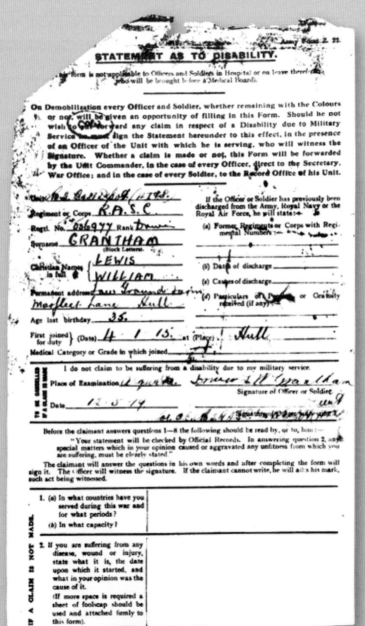

Army Form Z. 22.

STATEMENT AS TO DISABILITY.

This form is not applicable to Officers and Soldiers in Hospital or on leave therefrom who will be brought before a Medical Board.

On Demobilization every Officer and Soldier, whether remaining with the Colours or not, will be given an opportunity of filling in this Form. Should he not wish to put forward any claim in respect of a Disability due to Military Service he must sign the Statement hereunder to this effect, in the presence of an Officer of the Unit with which he is serving, who will witness the Signature. Whether a claim is made or not, this Form will be forwarded by the Unit Commander, in the case of every Officer, direct to the Secretary, War Office; and in the case of every Soldier, to the Record Office of his Unit.

COPY

Unit: [illegible] (H.T.S.)

Regiment or Corps: R.A.S.C.

Regtl. No.: 036977 Rank: Dvr.

Surname (Block Letters): GRANTHAM

Christian Names in full: LEWIS WILLIAM

Permanent address: New Ground Farm, Marfleet Lane, Hull

Age last birthday: 35.

First joined for duty (Date): 4 1 15. at (Place): Hull

Medical Category or Grade in which joined: A.

If the Officer or Soldier has previously been discharged from the Army, Royal Navy or the Royal Air Force, he will state:—

(a) Former Regiments or Corps with Regimental Numbers

(b) Date of discharge

(c) Causes of discharge

(d) Particulars of Pension or Gratuity received (if any)

TO BE CANCELLED IF A CLAIM IS MADE

I do not claim to be suffering from a disability due to my military service.

Place of Examination: [illegible] Driver L W Grantham

Signature of Officer or Soldier.

Date: 12 5 19.

[illegible]

Signature of Officer witnessing

Before the claimant answers questions 1—8 the following should be read by, or to, him:—

"Your statement will be checked by Official Records. In answering question 2, any special matters which in your opinion caused or aggravated any unfitness from which you are suffering, must be clearly stated."

The claimant will answer the questions in his own words and after completing the form will sign it. The Officer will witness the signature. If the claimant cannot write, he will affix his mark, such act being witnessed.

IF A CLAIM IS NOT MADE.

1. (a) In what countries have you served during this war and for what periods? (b) In what capacity?	
2. If you are suffering from any disease, wound or injury, state what it is, the date upon which it started, and what in your opinion was the cause of it. (If more space is required a sheet of foolscap should be used and attached firmly to this form).	

I will also mention Lewis's brother Harry Robinson. He was born in 1887, 3 years after Lewis. By the age of 14 Harry was a servant on a farm in the Burton Constable area nearby his home village of Aldbrough.

I think Harry must have had the "wish for adventure, excitement and pastures new" syndrome which affects some of us Granthams. Their elder brother Charlie had taken himself off to Canada in 1903, where he married and had 12 children. His grandchildren and great grandchildren still live there and also in Florida.

Anyway back to Harry. On the very day of his 18th birthday in 1905 he enlisted in the Royal Navy for a period of 12 years. He was on a number of different ships and took part in the Battle of Jutland in 1916.

Sadly on the 9th July 1917 at the age of 30, he was killed when his battleship, The Vanguard, exploded whilst at anchor near Flotta, Scapa Flow in the Orkneys. It is believed that the store of cordite caught fire causing an enormous explosion taking the lives of over 800 men.

His name is on the Chatham Naval Memorial and also on the war memorial in the village of Aldbrough.

In Memory of

Able Seaman

Harry Robinson Grantham

228054, H.M.S. "Vanguard.", Royal Navy who died on 09 July 1917

Remembered with Honour
Chatham Naval Memorial

Commemorated in perpetuity by
the Commonwealth War Graves Commission

Lewis the Proud Father and Soldier.

Lewis, Kate and firstborn Arthur Edward, taken in 1915.

Baking Powder Bread
1 lb Flour
½ oz Baking Powder
1 Teaspoon Salt
Cold water to mix.

Lentil Soup
1 Pint of Lentils
3 ½ Pints of Water or Stock
1 Large Carrot
½ Small Turnip
1 Large Potato or ½ oz Flour.
2 Teaspoons of Salt
3 Shakes Pepper.

Oatmeal Porridge
2 oz Oatmeal
1 pint Boiling Water
½ Teaspoonful Salt.

Measures

1 Tablespoon	1 oz.
1 Dessertspoon	½ oz
1 Teaspoon	¼ oz
1 Teacup	4 oz
1 Breakfast cup	6 oz
1 Large Tumbler	½ Pint
1 oz fat	The size of a Walnut.

Baking Powder
4 oz Carbonate Soda
3 oz Tartaric Acid
¼ lb Ground Rice.

Suet Dumplings
1 lb Flour
¼ lb Suet   1 Teaspoon Baking Powder
½ Teaspoonful Salt   Cold Water to Mix.

Cakelike Pudding

1 lb Flour
¼ lb Dripping
1 teaspoon B.P
2 oz sugar
¼ lb Currants
A little Spice
¼ Teaspoon Salt Water

Boiled Meat

Allow 20 minutes to each lb and 20 minutes over.

Fresh Meat

Plunge into boiling water. Boil 5 minutes.
Remove scum. Simmer until cooked.

Salt Meat

Place in cold water. Bring to boil. Skim. Simmer gently.
Cool in liquor.

Ham.

Soak all night. Scrape before boiling. 20 minutes 20 m over.

Fermented Bread

8 lb Flour
2oz Yeast
1 Teaspoon Sugar,
1 Tablespoon Salt 1 oz
Tepid Water   1 part boiling 2 parts cold
Warm the flour Add the salt
Test the yeast with the sugar
Mix to a fairly stiff dough with the yeast and tepid water
Knead with the palm of the hand
Put to rise for ½ hour
Bake in a hot oven at first then allow only a moderate heat
When the bread is done it should sound hollow.

Tomato Soup
1 lb Tomatoes
½ oz Sugar
1 Large Onion
1 Large Carrot
3 Pints Stock
1 oz Dripping
1 oz Flour
Seasoning

Irish Stew
1 lb scrag or middle neck of Mutton
Vinegar
2 lb Potatoes
½ lb Onions
Seasoning
1 Pint Boiling Water

Pease Pudding
1 lb Split Peas
4 Pints Water
2 oz Dripping or Butter
Seasoning

Boiled Fruit
1 lb Fruit
½ Pint Water
2 oz Sugar (or to taste)
Boil sugar and water. The fruit to be put in after.

Milk Pudding
2 oz Rice
1 oz Sugar
1 Pint Milk
Nutmeg
Pinch of salt
A little butter

Fig Pudding
¼ lb Flour
¼ lb Breadcrumbs
½ Teaspoon Baking Powder
2oz Figs chopped
2 oz Sugar
2 oz Suet
Grated Nutmeg
Water to mix. Fairly stiff
2 to 2 ½ hours

Rules for Frying
Frying is cooking in hot fat.
The pan should be heated for fatty foods.
The fat should have a faint blue smoke rising,
Frying is a suitable method for cooking small pieces of tender food.
e.g Sausages, Fish and Bacon.

Coffee
½ oz Coffee
1 Pint Boiling Water
Pinch of Salt

Warm a jug or can
Put coffee and salt in
Pour over quite boiling water
Pour out a cup and return twice
Stand ten minutes
Keep hot.

Fruit Pies
Any Fruit
Sugar to taste
A little water for the juice
16 oz Flour
4 oz Dripping
1 Teaspoonful Baking Powder
Pinch of Salt
Cold water to mix

Rules for making Short Pastry
Put the fat in the flour with the tips of fingers.
Keep everything as cool as possible.
Mix to a stiff paste with cold water.
Roll evenly and lightly.
Bake in a hot oven.

Roasting is cooking in front of a clear bright fire by direct heat
from it.
Baking is cooking in the oven in a tin.
Weigh and wipe the meat.
Allow the meat to cook quickly for the first ten minutes to harden
the outside and to keep in the juices then allow to cook gently
until done.
The meat should be constantly basted to keep it moist and prevent
it shrinking.
Allow for beef and mutton 15 minutes to the lb and 15 minutes
over.
Allow for pork and veal 20 minutes to the lb and 20 minutes
over.

Sultana Cake

½ lb Flour
3 oz Fat
2 oz Sugar
1 Egg
Milk to mix
1 Teaspoonful Baking Powder
Pinch of Salt
A little Spice
2 oz cleaned Sultanas or Currants
½ oz Candid Peel
1 hour ½

Rules for Cake Baking

Collect and prepare all ingredients and utensils.
Small cakes bake in hot oven 10 or 15 minutes.
Large cakes place in hot part of oven for 10 minutes, finish in a moderate oven.
When time allowance is up test with a skewer or needle. If clean the cake is done.
There are two kinds of cake mixture (rich) (plain).

1. Fat rubbed into the flour.
2. Fat and sugar creamed together. These need extra careful baking.

Rules for Frying Fish
Prepare the fat
Thoroughly dry and coat fish before cooking
Fatty fish e. g herrings and sprats require no fat in pan only a sprinkle of salt.

The Refuse Tub
If possible made of a non porous material e. g a bath or pail otherwise ½ filled with hay.
Refuse must be burned or buried at least once a day.

Bread Pudding
4 oz Soaked Bread
2 oz Currants
2 oz Sugar
1 Egg or a little milk
Nutmeg

Meat Pudding
Cooked Meat
Seasoning
½ Teaspoonful Mixed Herbs
½ Small Onion
8 oz Flour
2 oz Suet
½ Teaspoonful Baking Powder
Pinch Salt
Cold water to mix
If cooked meat cook for 2 hours, If raw 4 hours.

Shepherd's Pie
Cooked Potatoes
Cooked Meat
½ Small Onion
Seasoning
½ Teaspoonful Mixed Herbs
Gravy or Sauce

Reheating Cooked Food

Reheat but do not recook

Protect the meat with a covering of pastry, suet crust, sauce, batter or potatoes.

Season well. Use gravy or sauce not water.

Serve thoroughly hot.

Advantages of reheated food

It is more appetising.

It is more economical.

A greater variety of dishes can be obtained.

Rules for cooking Smoked Meats

If very dry or salty soak for 12 hours in cold water and scrape well.

Put into cold water. Add a little carb soda, sugar and spices.

Boil gently, skim frequently. Allow 20 minutes to each lb and 20 minutes over for thick pieces.

Allow to cool in liquor.

Serve cold sliced thinly.

Fruit in Batter
8 oz Flour
Pinch Salt or 1 Dessertspoon of Vinegar
1 or 2 Eggs
½ Teaspoon Carb of Soda
¾ Pint Milk
¼ Pint Water
Dripping
2 oz Raisins or any Fresh Fruit in season

Rules for Batter Making
Beat it well to get the air in.
Let it stand if possible 1 hour or longer to allow the starch grains to swell.
This makes it lighter.
Cook in a hot oven about 20 minutes.

Scones
½ lb Flour
½ Teaspoon Tartaric Acid   or 1 Teaspoon
¼ Teaspoon Carb Soda   of Baking Powder
Pinch of Salt
Milk to mix
Little Currants or Sultanas may be used.
When sour or buttermilk is used omit the acid.

Fried Tomatoes
Hot Fat
Halved or sliced Tomatoes

Cocoa
1 oz good Cocoa
1 qt or pt Boiling Water (difficult to read)
Little cold milk to mix

1 Teacup Cocoa Pods
3 Pts Water
Simmer 2 days

Tinned foods
Useful in emergencies.
Too salty and over cooked to use frequently.
Making a variety e. g fruit and veg out of season.
Tins should not bulge.
Food turned from the tin immediately after opening.
Cake Shut in a tin with an apple
Milk Scald. Cover with muslin. Keep cool.

Tainted food and water is very injurious causing vomiting and
intestinal troubles.

Preservation of Food

Meat and Fish (uncooked)

Hang up and keep covered.

Cooked meat keeps better and dry keeps best,

Never leave flat on a dish, raise on a grid or substitute, sprinkle with pepper and cover from flies. Keep in a cool place free from dust.

Veg and fruits keep better uncooked and packed separately in a cool dry place.

Bread

Wrap in a cloth or enclose in a tin with a small ventilating hole.

Catering
By exercising forethought time, trouble and money are saved.

Points to be considered when planning meals.
Number of persons to be fed.
Occupation of such persons.
Money to be expended.
Stove and utensils available.
Time for preparation.
Season.

Force meat suitable for stuffing Beef, Mutton, Veal and Fowl.
3oz Breadcrumbs or scraps of Stale Bread
1 oz Dripping or Butter
1 Tablespoonful Chopped Parsley
¼ Teaspoon Mixed Herbs
Seasoning
A little Milk or Egg

Sage and Onion Stuffing suitable for stuffing Pork or Mutton
2 Boiled Onions Chopped
3 oz Breadcrumbs
1 Teaspoonful Dried Sage
Seasoning

Rissoles

½ lb Cooked Meat (minced)
½ lb Breadcrumbs
1 Tablespoonful Chopped Parsley
1 teaspoonful Mixed Herbs
Seasoning
1 oz Fat or Suet
Egg or Egg and Milk to bind
Flour, Egg and Crumbs for coating

Meat Cakes

½ lb meat. Cold. Cooked
½ lb Cooked Mashed Potatoes
Seasoning
1 Teaspoonful Mixed Herbs (if liked)

Rock Cakes

½ lb Flour
1 Teaspoonful B. Powder
2 oz Currants
2 oz Sugar
1 Egg and Milk to mix stiffly
A little Nutmeg.

Digestibility

Food is cooked to render it digestible and make it more easily converted into body building material and to generate heat and energy. Starchy foods are useless in the body if uncooked. If improperly cooked cause pain as they lie in the body fermenting.

If waste is not repaired the body gets out of condition, becomes limp and subject to all known ailments.

The body is constructed to deal with a certain amount of excess in food e.g the kidneys expel excess in protein, the liver stores up sugar, the lymphatics store fat using it as a lubricant.

Hay Box Cookery

Dishes	Time on Stove	Time in Box
Stock	Boiling Point	All Night
Soup (Lentil etc)	¾ Hour	4 Hours
Fish Stewed in milk. Boiled in water	Boiling Point	½ Hour
Meat Beef Stew with Vegetables.	5 minutes (potatoes) ¾ Hour	4 Hours
Irish Stew.	¾ Hour (meat)	3 Hours
Vegetables Potatoes	5 minutes	2 ½ Hours
Haricot Beans soaked	1 Hour	3 Hours
Puddings Boiled Rice	Boiling Point	2 ½ Hours
Stewed Apples	Boiling Point	2 ½ Hours
Stewed Prunes	Boiling Point	2 ½ Hours
No Soaking		3 ½ Hours
Suet Pudding 4 oz	½ Hour	1 ½ Hours
Porridge Coarse Oatmeal	Boling Point	1 ½ Hours
Quaker Oat	Boiling Point	All Night

Army Rations

Table for finding quantities of food required for messing.

No of Men	Coffee for 1 Meal ozs	Tea 1 Meal ozs	Sugar 1 Meal lbs	Milk for Tea Coffee Pints	Oatmeal for Porridge lbs	Potatoes for Dinner lbs	Eggs
5	1 ½	1	½	½	½	4	10
10	3	2	½	1	1	8	20
20	6	4	1	2	2	12	40
30	8	6	1 ½	3	3	23	60
40	10	8	2	4	4	30	60
50	12	9 ½	2 ½	5	5	38	100
60	14	11	3	6	6	46	120
70	1 lb	12 ½	3 ½	7	7	54	140
80	1 1/8 lb	14	4	8	8	60	160
90	1 ¼ lb	15	4 ¼	9	9	68	180
100	1 3/8 "	1 lb	4 ½	10	10	75	200

Herrings, Bloaters, Small Haddock   1 per Man

Cheese lbs	Butter 1 Day lbs	Jam Marmalade lbs	Golden Syrup lbs	Brawn Bacon Sausages Mutton Chops lbs	Corned Beef Lunch Sausage lbs	Fish Salt Dried lbs	Liver or Steak lbs
½	5/16	¾	¾	1 ¼	1 ¼	2 ½	1 ¼
1	10/16	1 ¼	1 ½	2 ½	2	5	2 ½
1 ¾	1 ¼	2 ½	3	5	4	10	5
2 ½	1 ¾	3 ¾	4 ½	7 ½	6	15	7 ½
3 ¼	2 ½	5	6	10	8	20	10
4	3 ¼	6 ¼	7	12 ½	10	25	12 ½
4 ½	3 ¾	7 ½	8	15	12	30	15
5	4 ½	8 ½	9	17 ½	14	34	17 ½
5 ½	5	9 ½	10	20	16	38	20
6	5 ½	10 ½	11	22 ½	18	42	22 ½
6 ½	6 ¼	11 ½	12	25	20	45	25

Statement of Field Rations Received and Issued

Rations of	Brought Forward	Drawn	Total	Issued	Balance carried Forward	
Bread						
Meat						
Flour						
Biscuit						
Tea						
Jam						
Sugar						
Vegetables						
Salt						
Pepper						
Bacon						
Cheese						
Mustard						
Suet						
Dripping						

Food Purchased

Article	Quantity		Rate	£	S	D
	lbs	ozs	Rate	£	S	D
Flour	14				3	7
Sugar	2				1	2
Meat	6				7	11
Bacon	1				2	6
Tea	1	8			4	6
1 Bag Coals	120				3	10
Candles	2					2
Matches						11
Dried Fruit	1				1	2
Yeast						2
Baking P.	½					
Jam	1				1	8
Milk					2	7 ½
Rent					3	
G R Cn					1	7
Insurance						10

Macaroni Cheese

2 oz Macaroni	Washed and boiled 15 Minutes.
1 oz Fat	Melt the fat.
1 oz Flour	Add the flour to make a white sauce,
½ pt Milk	
Seasoning	
2 oz Grated Cheese	
Bread Crumbs	

Welsh Rarebit

Buttered Toast	
2 oz Cheese	Grated, put in sauce pan, add a little butter.
A Little Butter	
Seasoning	
Mustard	

Cheese

This well known food consists of the pressed and dried curds of milk. By adding rennet the nitrogenous substance called casein is used to coagulate and curdle it.

Curry of Cold Meat
Cooked Meat
1 pt Stock or Water
1 Dessertspoon Curry Powder
2 oz Dripping or Butter
1 small Onion
1 small Apple
¼ teaspoon Salt
Lemon juice or Vinegar

Boiled Rice
6 oz Rice
Boiling Water
Lemon or Vinegar
Salt

Beef Tea
½ lb Gravy Beef
½ pt Cold Water
Pinch Salt

Advantages of Bottled Fruit.
Obtainable at all seasons.
Can be kept for a long time.

<u>Lemon Curd</u>   to be made and used at once.
1 Teacup fine white sugar
1 Egg
Bit of Butter
Juice of 1 lemon
Grease the tin, beat the sugar and egg, then add juice. Beat again
then add the butter. Stir till it thickens.

<u>Ginger Buns</u>
5 oz Flour
Pinch Salt
1 ½ oz Lard
4 oz Treacle
1 ½ oz Sugar
¼ Teaspoon Bicarb Soda
½ Teaspoon Ground Ginger
1 Teaspoon Egg Powder
A Little Milk
Rub fat into flour, mix sugar, salt and egg powder. Add treacle
and beat well.
Mix soda in milk.
Beat together and put in tins.
Grease the tins before using.
Bake for 20 minutes.

<u>Pie</u>   (This seems a very strange recipe for a pie)
4 oz Mustard
4 oz Cornflour
1 oz Pepper
1 oz Ginger
4 oz Mustard Seed
4 oz Salt
½ oz Turmeric
½ lb Brown Sugar
3 ½ Quarts Vinegar   Q m G R (Do not know what this means)

Brown Sauce

1 Pt Stock
1 Onion   Fry the onion in the fat.
1 Carrot   Small
1 Turnip   Cut very small.
2 oz Flour
2 oz Fat
Seasoning

Fried Liver and Onions

½ lb Ox Liver   Cut in slices. Dip in S. Flour.
½ lb Onions   Fry the onions in the fat.
2 Tablespoon Seasoned Flour
2 oz Fat

Raspberry Buns

½ lb Flour
2 oz Fat
2 oz Sugar
1 Teaspoonful Tartaric
½ teaspoonful Carb of Soda
1 Egg
Little Milk
Stiff Paste
Little Raspberry Jam. 20 Minutes

Milk Sauce
½ Pint Milk
Yolks of 2 Eggs   Beat the eggs.
1 Teaspoonful Flour   Add the flour
Sugar to taste   Then the milk

Mayonaise
The Yolks of 2 Eggs
6 Tablespoonfuls of Salad Oil
4   "   "   "   Vinegar
Salt and Pepper
1 Tablespoonful of White Stock
2 Tablespoonfuls of Cream

Health Salts
½ lb Caster Sugar
2 oz Epsom Salts
2oz Cream Tarter
2 oz Tartaric Acid
2 oz Carb Soda

The Later Years.

Lewis and Kate in 1959.

The following photographs were very kindly supplied by the re-enactors of The Great War Society.
They show the kind of equipment and uniforms used during the Great War.

Stores and Supplies

A Field Kitchen

A.S.C Cooks

A Brew Up in the Trench

Some Heavy Duty Gardening

A Well Earned Ration Break

A Gas Cloud at Loos

Thoughtful Contemplation

THE GREAT WAR SOCIETY

The Great War Society is a non-profit making organisation based in the U.K.

*F*ounded in 1984, we provide an opportunity for practical research into the uniforms, weapons, equipment, training & everyday tasks of the Great War soldier. Our members dress in period uniforms & equipment, learn the drill and undertake the training and everyday activities of the time. We are a living-history group, not a battle re-enactment group - we feel it is neither possible, nor desirable to attempt to portray actual combat in front of the public. Rather, our activities are focused on authentic demonstrations of the many & various skills which a soldier would have to acquire to enable him to do his job in the field.

All of our uniform, equipment & weaponry is 100% accurate for the 1914-1918 period & our aim is to provide a living link with our Great War heritage - not merely current day people "in costume", but a living, breathing, authentic portrayal of the soldiers of the time which is as close as one can get to actually seeing & meeting them almost a century ago.

The Great War Society attends numerous events both in the UK & on the Western Front during the course of the year, for a variety of sponsors - these include English Heritage, The

Many of our events are in support of service charities, such as the Royal British Legion Poppy Appeal, Help for Heroes & the Soldiers Sailors, Airmen and Families Association (SSAFA), thus taking full account of the important link between the sacrifice of our Great War armed forces & those of the present day.

Our work on the Western Front includes commemorative marches in full kit & parades at various venues in France & Belgium. We have paraded officially at many high profile venues including the Menin Gate, the Thiepval Memorial, Tyne Cot Cemetery & Fromelles, to name but a few. Great War Society troops have also had the honour of parading at the reburials of Great War soldiers whose identified remains have been found on the Western Front.

As well as public displays and arena demonstrations as part of our national programme, the GWS has much experience in tailor-made presentations to private bodies. These include the British Army (Regular, TA & the Royal Military Academy Sandhurst), regimental museums & associations, plus schools & Army Cadet units.

The Great War Society is also occasionally called upon to act as a source of specialist military extras for film & TV productions. In this role, we are able to help

Sadly, the men & women who served our country during the Great War have now all passed away - however, over the years, we have forged firm friendships with many Great War soldiers, including "the Last Fighting Tommy", Harry PATCH, who accepted Honorary Veteran Membership of the GWS in 2004. These veterans have always been fully supportive of our activities in keeping alive the memory of their service during the 1914-1918 conflict. In recent years, though, it has been our sad duty & honour to have paraded at the funeral of one of the last Great War veterans, Albert "Smiler" MARSHALL, as well as having been in official uniformed attendance at the funeral of Harry PATCH.

We exist purely to educate the public, & to perpetuate the memory & highlight the sacrifices of the personnel who fought & served in "the war to end all wars" - sacrifices of life, of limb & of mind, which helped to secure the lives & liberties which we enjoy to this very day.

www.thegreatwarsociety.com